YOU ARE

A 31 Day Family Devotional

Rebekah Price

The characters and events portrayed in this book are fictitious. Any similarity to real persons, living or dead, is coincidental and not intended by the author.

ISBN-13: 9798643841609
ISBN-10: 1477123456

Cover design by: Kid Graphic
Library of Congress Control Number: 2018675309
Printed in the United States of America

I dedicate this book to my loving husband, Josh, and to my four wonderful sons, Tyler, Logan, Caden, and Tegan Hawke. You light up my life and bring me more joy than I could ever explain. I thank God for blessing me with you. I love you all!

CONTENTS

FOREWORD

You Are, by Rebekah Price, is a positive, faith-filled, month long family devotional designed to challenge families to draw closer to God as they discover who they are in Christ. The Bibical principles taught in this inspired devotional are simple enough for younger children to grasp and will engage and encourage older children to explore and deepen their relationship with God.

~ Eddie Smith, senior pastor of Faith Family Church, Jefferson, SC

DAY 1

YOU ARE CHOSEN

"But God chose you to be His people. You are royal priests. You are a holy nation. You are a people who belong to God. All of this is so that you can sing His praises."

1 Peter 2:9 NIRV

You should feel like the luckiest boy/girl in the world! God chose you! You may be thinking there's a lot of other people in the world. That's true, but God created you. He could've created anyone, but He chose to create you. You must be a pretty cool kid!

You were created to have a relationship with God. He wants to talk to you. He'll listen to you better than your best friend will. He'll never turn His back on you. You get to know Him by spending time with Him. Read the Bible. The Bible is like a big instruction manual for life. The more you read it, the more you know God; and the better your life will become.

You were chosen by God, so that means you have a purpose. Another word for purpose is the word plan. God has a plan for your life. You may have heard it said before that you could be anything you want to be. That's not entirely true. You can, but if you don't find out God's plan for your life, you will never be truly happy. That statement should say, "You can be anything that God wants you to be." God's plan for our life is always better than anything we could plan for ourselves.

Prayer for Child: Dear Heavenly Father, I thank You for choosing me, and in return I choose You. I'm thankful for my life. I commit to spending time with You by reading my Bible and talking to You daily. I know that You have a plan for my life, and I thank you that I will fulfill my purpose. In Jesus name, Amen.

Prayer for Parent: Dear Heavenly Father, I thank You for choosing me. I also thank you for choosing me to be the parent of (insert child's name__________.) I thank You for helping me to guide my child in Your ways so they may fulfill your purpose for their lives. In Jesus name, Amen.

DAY 2

YOU ARE LOVED

"For God loved the world so much that He gave His one and only Son. Anyone who believes in Him will not die, but will have eternal life."

John 3:16 NIRV

"No one has greater love, than the one who gives his life for his friends."

John 15:13 NIRV

Would you be willing to die for your friends? I love my friends, but I really wouldn't want to have to lay down my life for theirs. It seems a little unfair that someone has to die so that another can live. But Jesus did that for us. God wanted us to live with Him forever. He created Adam and Eve. Adam and Eve disobeyed God, and let sin come into the world. When they did, Satan took authority over man, and man was separated from God.

Think of it like this. Your Mom and Dad give you an iPod for your birthday. You love it! They tell you to take care of it and not take it to school. One day you decide to take your iPod to school, even though your parents told you not to. A classmate named Steve, who is a smooth talker, really wants to hold it and promises he won't break it. You know you shouldn't, but you let Steve hold it because he's one of the "cool" kids. As soon as he has it in his hands, he runs to the bathroom and throws it in the toilet. You are extremely mad at him but more upset that you disobeyed your parents. You go home and tell your parents knowing that you're in big trouble. Your Mom and Dad are disappointed in you. They thought that you would've obeyed them and heeded their warning. They forgive you, but to get another iPod, you'll have to pay the price, $250.00. It looks like your lemonade stand isn't going to cut it.

Just like you would have to pay the price to get a new iPod, God had to pay the price to get man back. Jesus was that price. God loved us so much that He was willing to give His only Son. Jesus loved us so much that he died for us. Jesus is the best older brother ever!

Prayer for Child: Dear Heavenly Father, I thank you for loving me so much that you sent your only Son to die for me. I'm so thankful that I get to be your child and one day live with You. In Jesus name, Amen.

Prayer for Parent: Dear Heavenly Father, I thank you for your love for my family and me. I thank you for Jesus. I thank you that Jesus took my place. I know that I am to be a mirror of You. I ask you to help my children see Your love for them through me. In Jesus name, Amen.

DAY 3

YOU ARE LOVING

"I give you a new command. Love one another. You must love one another, just as I have loved you. If you love one another, everyone will know that you are my disciples."

John 13:34 NIRV

If you're like most people, then you probably love your Mom, Dad, brothers, sisters, Grandparents, and the rest of your family. Maybe you love your best friend, a dog, a cat, or whatever pet you own. I bet all these people/pets are easy to love (most of the time) because they love you. You like being around them. You don't mind helping them out because you love them. But what about the people that aren't so lovable?

Jill was so excited because it was the first day of cheerleading tryouts. She had spent all summer learning how to do a cart-wheel and a split so that she could make the squad. She knew a couple of the girls on the squad, and she was eager to meet the rest. The captain of the squad, Brandy, who was a year older than Jill, walks into the gym with her head held high and nose in the air. She was there to watch the tryouts. Finally, it was Jill's turn. She nervously performed her cheers, jumps, splits, and cart-wheel. Just as she was finishing her cart-wheel, she heard hysterical laughing. Brandy was doubled over laughing! "You call that a cart-wheel?" Brandy mocked. Jill's face turned red, and she ran out of the gym. She was so embarrassed!

I'm sure Jill probably had some mean thoughts about Brandy after that incident. Do you think she could love Brandy after that? I'm sure you can think of some people who have done mean things to you. As a Christian, God commands you to love all people. No matter how they act, you still love them. When you show love to someone who doesn't deserve it, it changes them. It also changes you because you don't let them have control over you anymore. God said that if you love people, people would know that you belong to Him. I want people to know that I'm His child. It starts with loving people.

Prayer for Child: Dear Heavenly Father, I ask You to help me to love people the way that You do. I choose to love everyone, even the people who aren't loving. I thank You, Father, that everyone knows that I am Your child because of the way I show love. In Jesus name, Amen.

Prayer for Parents: Dear Heavenly Father, I ask You to help me to love people the way You do. I ask You to help me to be an example of your love for my children. Help my family show love to each other and everyone around us. In Jesus name, Amen.

CHALLENGE: Read 1 Corinthians 13 to get a better understanding of what love really is. After you read it, write in your own words or draw a picture of what it means to show God's love.

DAY 4

YOU ARE IN CONTROL OF YOUR EMOTIONS

"But the fruit the Holy Spirit produces is love, joy, and peace. It is being patient, kind and good. It is being faithful and gentle and having control of oneself."

Galatians 5:22&23 NIRV

What are emotions? Another word for emotions is feelings. Have you watched the movie *Inside Out*? In the movie, an 11-year-old girl's five emotions, (joy, disgust, fear, anger, and sadness) try to guide her through a difficult transition after she moves from the Midwest to San Francisco. The movie shows how feelings can change based on what's going on around us. God wants us to know that we don't have to let our emotions rule us. Just the opposite, He wants us to be in charge of our emotions. God made us the boss over our bodies.

All emotions are not bad. Some emotions are good. Joy, hope, thankfulness, kindness, and cheerfulness are all good emotions that come from God. There are other emotions that the devil tries to send our way to cause us to be sad and not in control of our bodies.

I want you to pick up your hand and spread all your fingers out. Now, turn your hand sideways with your thumb on top. Your thumb represents you, and your fingers represent the emotions disgust, fear, anger, and sadness. You should always be on top of these emotions. Now, turn your hand upside down so that your thumb is on the bottom. These emotions should never be on top. When they are, they are controlling you.

How do we control our emotions? One way to control our emotions is by reading God's Word and believing what He says is true. Today's scripture says that God has given us self-control. That means that we can stay on top of our emotions. Another way to control your emotions is not to respond to a situation quickly. Take time to think about how you feel before you react. It's ok to have emotions, just don't let them rule you.

Prayer for Child: Dear Heavenly Father, I ask You to help me to be the boss of my feelings. I thank You for giving me self-control. I ask you to help me to use self-control in every part of my life. In Jesus name, Amen.

Prayer for Parent: Dear Heavenly Father, I ask You to help me be a master of my emotions. I thank You that I have self-control in every situation and every area of my life. I thank you that my children are learning not to let their emotions control them. In Jesus name, Amen.

CHALLENGE:

Older Child: Write about a situation when you controlled your emotions, or a time when you let your emotions control you.

Younger Child: Tell your Mom or Dad about something that makes you feel sad or mad. (Parent: talk to your child about how they can stay in control of their emotions in that situation.)

DAY 5

YOU ARE A WINNER

"But thanks be to God, who gives us the victory through our Lord Jesus Christ."

1 Corinthians 15:57 AMP

Winner- a person or thing that wins something.

If you have asked Jesus into your heart, then you are a winner because you are on the winning team. What are you winning? Life! God will cause you to come out on top in every situation if you put Him first.

KJ loved baseball! When he wasn't at school or church, you could find him in his backyard practicing with his brother. But the most important thing in KJ's life was Jesus. He loved to tell people about Jesus and was liked by all because of his love for people.

Baseball season had flown by, and it was the last game of the season. The bases were loaded, and KJ was up to bat. It was the last inning, and KJ had to bring a runner home if his team was going to win. KJ said a prayer under his breath, "Dear Lord, please help me to do my best and hit the ball. I need the strength of Samson." He laughed a little to himself, took a deep breath, and stepped up to the plate. Strike 1! Strike 2! KJ knew this could be his last pitch. The pitcher was throwing some nasty curveballs. On the third pitch, KJ swung with all his might. Ding! The ball went flying into the outfield! As KJ rounded third base, heading towards the plate, he hears someone in the stands call out, "KJ, wake up! It's time to get dressed for school." It was KJ's mom. He woke up and realized it was just a dream, but what a great dream it was.

I don't believe that God makes a team win because then he would have to make another team lose. Unless it's the UNC Tarheels, everyone knows that's God's favorite team. I'm just kidding! That's my favorite college team. So, while you may not hit the winning run of the game, you can still be a winner in life. If you strike out, you try again. Failure is not an option when God is on your side. Whatever situation you may face, God will cause it to work out for your good if you put your trust in Him.

Just remember, you can be all that God says you are. God calls you a winner!

Prayer for Child: Dear Heavenly Father, I ask you to help me see myself as you do. I thank you for making me a winner in life. In Jesus name, Amen.

Prayer for Parent: Dear Heavenly Father, I thank you for always causing me to have victory through Jesus. I ask you to help me always to make my children feel like they are winners. In Jesus name, Amen.

Challenge:

Older Child: Is there an area in your life that you feel like you are not winning? Write out a game plan to help you start being victorious in that area. Example: If you are getting bad grades in school, come up with things you can do to improve your grades. Study for test, get a tutor, talk to your teacher, etc.

Younger Child: Draw a picture of you receiving a trophy and copy today's memory verse under your picture.

DAY 6

YOU ARE SLOW TO ANGER

"My dear brothers and sisters, pay attention to what I say. Everyone should be quick to listen. But they should be slow to speak. They should be slow to get angry. A man's anger doesn't produce the kind of life God wants."

James 1:19-20 NIRV

If you're alive and breathing, then I'm sure you've been angry before. What makes you angry? It could be that your sister ate the last pop- tart and you called it. Or, you wanted to go to Nick's house for the weekend, and your mom said no. People get mad for lots of reasons. You may feel that you have a right to be mad when things don't go your way, but the scripture above says that we are to be slow to anger. That means that we shouldn't be quick to get mad.

Zoe's church had started a new reward system for bringing your Bible and memorizing scripture verses. The kids earned points that could be used at the church store to buy prizes. Zoe had her eye on a heart-shaped necklace and had been saving her points for months. She finally had earned the points to buy the necklace. That Sunday morning, Zoe jumped out of bed and dressed quickly. She couldn't wait to get to church. Finally, it was time for the store to open, and Zoe anxiously awaited her turn. Zoe was next in line when she heard Becky, who was in front of her, say, "I want that necklace." It was the necklace that Zoe had been saving to buy! Zoe could feel her face turn red and heat rush through her body. "That's my necklace!" Zoe proclaimed. Before she thought, she snatched the necklace out of Becky's hand. Becky, who was three years younger than Zoe, began to cry. The teacher looked at Zoe and exclaimed, "Zoe, that was not nice! If you would've waited your turn, I would've told you that we have two more necklaces just like that." Zoe was embarrassed and sorry for how she had acted. She had let her anger get the best of her and reacted without thinking. Zoe apologized to Becky, and thankfully Becky forgave her.

The next time that you have an opportunity to get angry, remember that God says you should be slow to anger. Ask yourself this, will it matter in 10 years, next week, or tomorrow? You'll find that a lot of times we are tempted to get mad at things that aren't a big deal. Before you respond in anger, take a deep breath, and count to ten. Then, pray and ask the Lord to help you. A calmness will come over you and help you respond in a way that is pleasing to the Lord.

Prayer for Child: Dear Heavenly Father, I ask you to help me to be quick to listen, slow to speak, and slow to get angry. In Jesus name, Amen.

Prayer for Parent: Dear Heavenly Father, I ask you to help me to be quick to listen, slow to speak, and slow to get angry. I ask you to help me to respond to every situation the way that you would. In Jesus name, Amen.

Challenge: Read Proverbs 15:18, Proverbs 16:32 and Proverbs 19:11.

DAY 7

YOU ARE FULL OF JOY

"May the God who gives hope, fill you with great joy."

Romans 15:13a NIRV

"Those who do right can expect joy."

Proverbs 10:28 NIRV

"I've got the joy, joy, joy, joy down in my heart. Where? Down in my heart. Where? Down in my heart." I remember singing this song when I was a child. It was one of my favorites. If you are a child of God, then you should have joy in your heart too. One of the definitions of joy is a feeling of great pleasure and happiness. God's children should be the happiest people on earth.

It was Christmas morning, and Liam and Ava were so excited to open their presents. Liam received the drum set that he had been wanting, and Ava got the dollhouse of her dreams. They were both very thankful and full of joy. It had been the best day ever.

Everyone likes to get presents. Getting presents makes you joyful. It's a good thing to give to the people you love; but you can have joy in your everyday life, not just on special days. The joy that you have should come from knowing that God loves you and that you're His child. God doesn't want you to be sad or in a bad mood. He wants you to be happy. Happiness is a decision. You can choose to be happy, or you can choose to be sad. Choose to be full of joy! I promise your life will be much better if you do.

Prayer for Child: Dear Heavenly Father, I ask you to fill me with joy. I choose happiness over sadness. In Jesus name, Amen.

Prayer for Parent: Dear Heavenly Father, I ask you to fill me with joy. I thank You that your joy is my strength. I thank you that you make me a happy parent and that I won't succumb to the emotions of the day. In Jesus name, Amen.

Challenge: The Bible says that laughing does the body good. It also produces joy. It's hard to be sad when you're laughing.

Here's a joke for you. Q. Why did the student eat his homework? A. Because his teacher told him it was a piece of cake.

Take turns telling your favorite jokes.

DAY 8

YOU ARE PATIENT

"Better a patient person than a warrior, one with self-control than one who takes a city."

Proverbs 16:32 NIV

We live in a fast-paced world. If we want to talk to a friend, we shoot them a text and usually get an instant response. Hungry? No problem! Pop a frozen waffle in the toaster, and it'll be ready in 2 mins. Want to watch your favorite cartoon? There's no need to wait until it's scheduled time, go to Netflix and find the episode you want to watch. These luxuries are nice, but they don't teach us how to be patient.

Zeke loved the month of February. Most kids like February because they like getting chocolate on Valentine's Day, but Zeke had a better reason to love February. His birthday was February 24, and he loved getting presents. Zeke knew that his mom had ordered his present from her favorite online shopping site and that it was on the way to his house. When the Fed Ex truck arrived, Zeke peeked out of his window to see if he could tell what the package was. There was no writing on the outside box.

Later that evening, his mom and dad decided to go for a

walk and left Zeke at the house. Zeke knew he shouldn't, but he decided to go in his parent's closet and get his birthday present. He quickly opened the box and found the video game he had wanted. He squealed with delight. "Busted!", yelled Zeke's older brother. When Zeke's parents returned, they learned about what Zeke had done. They let Zeke keep his birthday present, but they told him he wouldn't be getting anything on the day of his birthday. His birthday was still two weeks away. When his birthday finally arrived, it felt just like an ordinary day.

Patience means waiting with a good attitude. Today's scripture says that a patient person is better than a warrior. Warriors are strong and take what they want, but God values a person that patiently waits for what is his.

Prayer for Child: Dear Heavenly Father, I ask you to help me to be patient in all that I do. In Jesus name, Amen.

Prayer for Parent: Dear Heavenly Father, I ask you to help me to be patient, especially in my parenting. Help me to be patient with my children just as you are patient with me. In Jesus name, Amen.

CHALLENGE: Today, you have a test. Practice patience! Remember, being patient is waiting with a good attitude. As you go about your day, make a conscious effort to be patient. Make a list of how many times you had an opportunity not to be patient. Grade yourself. Did you pass the test?

DAY 9

YOU ARE RESPONSIBLE

"Each one should test their own actions. They can take pride in themselves alone, without comparing themselves to someone else. For each one should carry their own load."

Galatians 6:4-5 NIV

Are you a responsible kid? You may be thinking that you don't know the answer to that question. Let me help you out. Do you keep your room clean without being told? Do you do your homework and turn it in on time? Do you read your Bible without having to be reminded? If the answer is yes, congratulations, you are a responsible kid! If the answer is no, don't worry because you can become a responsible kid.

Tessie and Jessie were twins. They shared the same love of softball, the same love of clothes, the same room, and the same chores. At least they were supposed to. Tessie was the more organized twin. She loved things to be in order. Her side of the room was always neat and clean. She always made sure she put her toys away and made her bed every day. She took care of her belongings. Jessie, on the other hand, was a hot mess! Her side of the room was always a disaster. She never put her toys away, and her sheets were almost always in a tangled mess, stuffed under her bed. She never could find her clothes because instead of putting them in her drawers, they landed wherever she threw them. One day the phone rang, and it was Tessie and Jessie's grandpa wanting to take them out for ice cream. Their mom took one look at their room and was horrified by Jessie's side of the room. While Tessie was rewarded and went with her grandpa, Jessie had to stay home and clean. Her lack of responsibility had cost her a fun trip with her grandpa.

Let's break today's scripture down. First, it reads that we should judge our actions. That means that if you know what to do, then do it. In Jessie's case, she should've seen that her room was a mess and cleaned it. This one step would have kept her from trouble.

The second part tells us that we can take pride in ourselves without comparing ourselves to someone else. Tessie probably had all of her drawers color-coded and knew how many of each article of clothing was in each drawer. Jessie should have cleaned her side of the room, but not felt like she had to do it Tessie's way.

The last line says that we should carry our load. That means we should take care of our responsibilities. Someone else shouldn't have to take care of their part and yours. It would not have been fair if Tessie had to clean the whole room by herself because Jessie wouldn't do her part.

So, I leave you with one question. Are you like Tessie or Jessie? If we're honest, we can probably say that we're a little of both. I'm sure Jessie has lots of good qualities, but she needed to learn to be responsible.

Prayer for Child: Dear Heavenly Father, I ask you to help me to do what I'm supposed to without being told. In Jesus name, Amen.

Prayer for Parent: Dear Heavenly Father, I ask you to help me be efficient in all my responsibilities. I ask you to give me the grace to finish each task. I also ask that you help me teach my children to be responsible for natural things so that they will become responsible for spiritual things. In Jesus name, Amen.

Challenge: Keep your room clean all week without your mom or dad telling you to clean it.

DAY 10

YOU ARE SUCCESSFUL

"Commit to the Lord everything you do. Then your plans will succeed."

Proverbs 16:3

Succeed: achieve the desired aim or result.

If you put God first, He will make you successful. That means that you'll always come out on top. God will help you thrive in school, with your friendships, and in your family. He'll cause everything you do to turn out well if you commit everything to Him.

Let's play a guessing game. Which fast food restaurant is famous for their chicken sandwich and waffle fries? If you guessed Chick-Fil-A, then you are right! The founder of Chick-Fil-A, Mr. Cathy, was a Christian man and believed that Sunday is the Lord's day. He never opened his restaurant on Sunday. Mr. Cathy passed away, but Chick-Fil-A still closes on Sunday. Mr. Cathy grew up in poverty and became a billionaire. He put God first, and God made him a very successful man. Chick-Fil-A is on track to become the third-largest fast-food chicken chain in the country!

There are things that you must do to become successful. You need to work with God. He will help you, but you must do your part. Mr. Kathy didn't become successful by sitting around and wishing that he owned a restaurant. No, he had a dream to make the best chicken sandwich, and he started taking steps toward that dream. It took hard work and probably many tries, but he didn't give up.

God will make you successful in big and small things. If you have a test and you want to make a good grade, then you must study the material and ask the Holy Spirit to remind you of what you studied. Are you feeling lonely? Start being friendly and ask the Lord to give you a friend. He will make your friendships successful. The things that are important to us are important to God.

Prayer for Child: Dear Heavenly Father, I give You everything. I ask you to guide me and cause me to succeed in every area of my life. In Jesus name, Amen.

Prayer for Parent: Dear Heavenly Father, I commit my life to you. In doing so, I know that you will cause my plans to succeed. I thank you that my child is a success going somewhere to manifest. In Jesus name, Amen.

Challenge: Tell a family member or friend about a time that the Lord caused you to be successful.

DAY 11

YOU ARE HIGHLY FAVORED

"For you, oh Lord bless the righteous man (the one who is in right standing with you) You surround him with favor as a shield."

Psalm 5:12 AMP

Do you have a favorite stuffed animal? Or a favorite blanket? What makes it your favorite? It could be the way it feels, smells, or maybe it reminds you of someone or something. Thankfully, God favors all His children and will cause you to have favor with other people too.

Care Bears was my favorite cartoon when I was young. One year for Christmas, my parents gave me a Care Bears sleeping bag and tent. I was so excited! I slept in the sleeping bag every night. I loved it so much that I gave it the name, Fluffly. Over the years, the tent got lost, but I kept the sleeping bag. It became ripped, and I outgrew it, but I refused to throw it away because it was my favorite. The reason I loved it so much was because of the way it made me feel. It was soft and comforting. If I had gotten in trouble, I would cry my tears into that blanket, and it would make me feel better. When I was cold, the blanket would keep me warm. I favored that blanket even though it hadn't done anything to deserve to be favored. Any other blanket could have kept me warm, but I didn't want another blanket, I wanted that one.

I'm sure your parents favor you over other people's children. Another kid may be nicer than you are at times, but your parent would still choose you because you are theirs and they love you. God favors us because we're His children. I'm God's favorite child! You're God's favorite child too!

Prayer for Child: Dear Heavenly Father, I'm so glad that I'm your favorite child. Thank you for loving me and shielding me with your favor. In Jesus name, Amen.

Prayer for Parent: Dear Heavenly Father, I thank you that I have favor with you. I ask you to give me favor with my boss and everyone that comes across my path. I ask you to give my child favor with their teachers and classmates. In Jesus name, Amen.

CHALLENGE: Read Psalm 35: 5, Psalm 35: 27, Acts 2:47, Acts 7:10, Genesis 19:19, Genesis 30:27 and Genesis 33:15 to learn more about God's favor.

DAY 12

YOU ARE HELPFUL

"Don't look out only for your own interest, but take an interest in others, too."

Philippians 2:4 NLT

Mark 10:45 NLT "For even the Son of Man came not to be served, but to serve others and to give His life as a ransom for many."

Mark 10:45 NLT

God wants us to have a servant's heart. When we have a servant's heart, we want to help others. The Bible says that Jesus came to serve people. Jesus is our example of how we should live our lives. If Jesus wasn't above serving others and saw it as an important part of life, then we should too.

Mrs. Carol was an elderly lady who was very active in her church and community. One day, while walking up the steps, she fell and broke her hip. Mrs. Carol was very upset because she didn't know how she was going to take care of her responsibilities around her house. Her husband had died three years earlier, and her children lived in a different state. Mrs. Carol felt all alone. The day she came home from the hospital, she was shocked to find her lawn mowed and a care package was sitting on her doorsteps. Inside the package was a sweet note from her church, letting her know that they were praying for her and that arrangements had been made for her lawn for the rest of the summer. God was taking care of Mrs. Carol by using people who had a servant's heart.

Sometimes we get so busy with our own lives, that we fail to help other people. God wants us to be helpful. If your brother misplaces his shoe, help him find it. If you see laundry that's unfolded, fold it. If we look around, there are always opportunities to be helpful.

Prayer for Child: Dear Heavenly Father, I ask you to give me a servant's heart. I want to be helpful and serve others the way that Jesus did. In Jesus name, Amen.

Prayer for Parent: Dear Heavenly Father, I ask you to forgive me for the times that I have looked the other way and not served people the way that I should've. I ask you to help me not to get so busy and wrapped up in my own life, that I forget to serve others. Give me a servant's heart. In Jesus name, Amen.

CHALLENGE: Plan an activity that involves serving others together as a family.

DAY 13

YOU ARE PROTECTED

"He who dwells in the shelter of the Most High will remain secure and rest in the shadow of the Almighty. I will say of the Lord, "He is my refuge and my fortress, My God in whom I trust!"

Psalm 91:1-2 AMP

One of my favorite Bible stories about God's protection is the story of Daniel and the Lion's Den. You can read the full story in Daniel 6.

King Darius had appointed 120 royal rulers over his entire kingdom. Then, he placed three leaders over them. One of the leaders was Daniel. The royal rulers were made accountable to the three leaders. The king did this so that no one would steal or misuse the wealth. Daniel did a better job than the other two leaders, so the king planned to put him in charge of the whole kingdom. This action angered the other two leaders, so they looked for a reason to bring charges against Daniel. They tried to find something wrong with the way he ran the government, but they couldn't find anything. Daniel could always be trusted. He never did anything wrong, and he always did what he was supposed to. So, the other two leaders came up with a plan to trick the king. They got the king to sign a law that said no one could pray to anyone except the king for the next 30 days and if they did, they would throw them into a den of hungry lions.

Daniel found out that the king had signed the law, but he did what he had always done. Three times a day, Daniel prayed to God in front of his window. When the other two leaders saw Daniel praying, they reported it to the King. The King was very upset because he didn't want to see Daniel harmed, but he knew his law couldn't be changed. Daniel was thrown into the lion's den, and the king said to him, "You have always served your God faithfully, so may He protect you!" And God did! He sent an angel to shut the mouths of the lions, and they didn't harm Daniel. Then the King made a new law decreeing that everyone had to serve the God of Daniel.

God protected Daniel, and God will protect you!

Prayer for Child: Dear Heavenly Father, I thank you for protecting me and keeping me safe from all harm. In Jesus name, Amen.

Prayer for Parent: Dear Heavenly Father, I thank you for your protection. I thank you for the angels encamped around my family and me. I thank you for keeping us safe and delivering us from all harm. In Jesus name, Amen.

CHALLENGE: Read Psalm 91 for a better understanding of God's protection.

DAY 14

YOU ARE HEALED

"Who Himself bore our sins in His own body on the tree, that we, having died to sins, might live for righteousness, by whose stripes you were healed."

1 Peter 2:24 NKJV

"That it might be fulfilled which was spoken by Esaias the prophet, saying, Himself took our infirmities, and bare our sicknesses."

Matthew 8:17

When Jesus was on the earth, he was a talked-about guy. People had never seen miracles performed until that time. In those days they didn't have the internet, tv, or the radio. People spread the news by talking to other people, aka gossiping. Jesus was healing people, and the news was traveling fast. He was the talk of the town and the countryside!

One of the Jewish leaders, Jairus, heard about Jesus healing the sick. His little girl became very ill and was on the verge of death. So, Jairus set out to find Jesus; but Jesus wasn't nearby. He had been teaching on the other side of the Sea of Galilee. When Jesus returned, Jairus begged him to come to his house and pray for her. Before Jesus could get to the house, someone came and told Jairus that his daughter had died. As soon as Jesus heard the words spoken, He looked at Jairus and said," Don't be afraid; only believe." When Jesus got to the house, he took the little girl by the hand and said to her, "Little girl, I say to you, arise." She immediately arose and walked. Then Jesus told the parents to get her something to eat. The little girl was no longer sick!

Jairus put his trust in Jesus, and we need to put our trust in Jesus. Hebrews 13:8 says that Jesus Christ is the same yesterday, today, and forever. That means that if Jesus healed Jairus' daughter, then he will heal you too. There's nothing too big or too small that God can't heal. When Jesus died on the cross for you, he died not only so that you could be saved; but he also died so that you could be healed. All we need to do is receive it. I'm so thankful that Jesus wants me well!

Prayer for Child: Dear Heavenly Father, I thank you that Jesus took my sicknesses for me, so there is no need for me to keep them. I accept what Jesus has given me. I thank you that by His stripes I am healed! In Jesus name, Amen.

Prayer for Parent: Dear Heavenly Father, I thank you that because Jesus took my infirmities and bore my sicknesses, there is no need for me to bare them. I accept what Jesus has provided for me. I thank you that by Jesus' stripes, I am healed! In Jesus name, Amen.

CHALLENGE: In Mark 16:18, Jesus said that believers would lay hands on the sick, and the sick would recover. If you come across someone not feeling good, lay your hands on them and pray for their body to get better. It doesn't matter if you are a child. God will honor your faith!

DAY 15

YOU ARE BRAVE

"For God has not given us a spirit of fear, but of power and of love and of a sound mind."

2 Timothy 1:7 NKJV

"There is no fear in love. Instead, perfect love drives fear away."

1 John 4:18 NIRV

Have you ever been so afraid that you couldn't move? Have you ever been so afraid that you peed in your pants? Yikes! Maybe you haven't ever been frozen with fear, and hopefully, you haven't peed in your pants; but everyone has experienced fear at some point in their life.

Timmy shared a room with his little brother. He pretended that he didn't like sharing a room with him, but secretly, he did. Timmy didn't want his own room because he was afraid of the dark. One day, his mom and dad had a big surprise for him. They cleaned out the basement so that he could have his own room. Timmy thanked them, but he was freaking out on the inside. That night as Timmy was lying in bed, he was overcome by fear. He was all alone, and it was dark. Very dark! Timmy was about to drift off to sleep when suddenly he heard a noise. It was a creaking noise coming from the stairs. Timmy could hear footsteps and heavy breathing and whatever or whoever was coming closer to him. He threw the covers over his head and tried to scream, but nothing would come out. He felt a hand pull the covers back and he knew he was a goner. He closed his eyes tight and hoped that this was a nightmare and that he would wake up soon. "Timmy, are you ok?", asked Mom. Timmy was so relieved that it was his mom and not a monster, that he threw himself into her arms.

There are a lot of different fears that people have. Some of the most common fears are fear of the dark, fear of monsters, fear of spiders, fear of heights, and the fear of death. Some people might tell you that it's normal to be fearful, but that's not what God says. God said that he didn't give you a spirit that would make you weak and fearful, but one of power and love. He also gave you a sound mind. That's a mind without scary thoughts.

The second scripture at the top says that perfect love drives fear away. That means that God loves you so much that His love drives fear away. You don't have to be scared! God makes you brave!

Prayer for Child: Dear Heavenly Father, I thank You that You have not given me a spirit of fear; but of power, love and a sound mind. I thank you that I'm not fearful of anything. I lie down, and my sleep is sweet. I thank you for making me brave. In Jesus name, Amen.

Prayer for Parent: Dear Heavenly Father, I thank You that You have not given me a spirit of fear; but of power, love, and a sound mind. I thank you that my children are free from fear. In Jesus name, Amen.

Challenge: Rent the movie Brave and make plans to have a popcorn and movie night sometime this week.

DAY 16

YOU ARE WISE

"The mouths of those who do what is right speak words of wisdom."

Psalm 37:30 NIRV

"If you really want to gain knowledge, you must begin by having respect for the Lord."

Proverbs 1:7 NIRV

Have you ever been around a group of your friends and they were saying mean things about someone else? If so, did you join in or did you have a scratchy feeling on the inside like that wasn't right? Maybe you even took up for that person. A wise person wouldn't have joined in that conversation. Wisdom is being able to know the difference between right and wrong.

God appeared to Solomon in a dream and asked him what He could give him. Solomon asked the Lord for wisdom. Solomon was called by God to do a big job as a young man. He was a King! He knew that he needed help in knowing how to be a good king and take care of the kingdom. Solomon's answer pleased God. His heart was good. He could've asked for anything, but he asked God for the most important gift. God blessed him with wisdom and made him a successful and prosperous king.

Solomon respected God, and in return, he gained wisdom. If you want to be a wise kid, then you need to respect God. When you respect God, you love him with your entire being! You put Him first. In return, He will give you wisdom.

Prayer for Child: Dear Heavenly Father, I love and respect you. I ask you to make me a wise kid. In Jesus name, Amen.

Prayer for Parent: Dear Heavenly Father, I love and respect you. I ask you to give me wisdom in every situation I face. I ask you to make me a wise parent. In Jesus name, Amen.

CHALLENGE: What animal is considered wise? Answer: Owl

Do you think the owl is wise? Discuss as a family. You may get some funny answers.

DAY 17

YOU ARE OBEDIENT

"Children obey your parents in the Lord, for this is right. Honor your father and mother, which is the first commandment with promise: that it may be well with you and you may live long on the earth."

Ephesians 6:1-3 NKJV

"Everyone must submit to governing authorities. For all authority comes from God, and those in positions of authority have been placed there by God."

Romans 13:1 NLT

We learn a very important lesson about obedience in the first book of the Bible, Genesis. God had one rule for Adam and Eve. Do you know what that rule was? That's right! He told them not to eat from the tree of the knowledge of good and evil. They had an entire garden of trees that provided food. That one tree was the only tree that was off-limits. Adam and Eve had everything they could want, but still, they chose to disobey God. Their disobedience cost them. They became separated from God. God no longer supplied everything for them. Adam had to work, and Eve felt pain when she had her babies. Disobedience is a sin. There is always a consequence for sin.

Logan and Tyler were brothers that loved to play baseball. Every day after school they would play catch in the yard. Their mom loved to see them playing with each other and having fun, but she had a rule about baseball. The rule was that baseballs were only to be played with outside and never thrown around windows. One rainy day, Tyler and Logan were bored. "Logan, go get the baseball and let's throw it.", said Tyler. "I don't want to get in trouble. What if we break something?", replied Logan. "Stop being a baby!" Tyler jeered. "Ok, but we have to be careful," said Logan. Tyler and Logan quietly threw the ball back and forth with no problem. "Back up some," encouraged Tyler. Logan took a couple of steps back. Logan had a bad feeling, but he didn't want to make his older brother upset. Tyler threw the ball, and Logan missed it. The ball hurled right smack through the window! Crash! Glass was everywhere! Their mom came running up the stairs and almost stepped on a piece of glass. Tyler and Logan were in big trouble because they had not obeyed their mom.

When you obey your parents and those in authority, it pleases God. God put people in charge of you not to make you mad, but to help you. Rules are made to protect you. You may not always understand the rules, but you still must follow them.

Adam and Eve thought it would be ok to eat just one piece of fruit. They didn't see what the big deal was, but it cost them everything. If you obey your parents, God said it would be well with you and that you would live long on the earth. So, if you want to have a good life and a long life, you must obey your parents.

Prayer for Child: Dear Heavenly Father, I ask You to help me to be obedient even when I don't feel like it. I thank you for my parents, teachers, and everyone that you have placed over me. In Jesus name, Amen.

Prayer for Parent: Dear Heavenly Father, I thank You that as I am obedient to You, my children will be obedient to You too. I thank you that my children are obedient to me and all authority figures. I ask You to help me to know when to show mercy and when to discipline them for their disobedience. In Jesus name, Amen.

CHALLENGE:

1. Find a person in the Bible that obeyed God and received a reward for his/her obedience.

2. Find a person in the Bible that disobeyed God and paid the price for his/her disobedience.

DAY 18

YOU ARE FOLLOWING GOD

"The Lord directs the steps of the godly. He delights in every detail of their lives."

Psalm 37:23 NLT

When God created you, He created you with a purpose. He has a special job that He wants you to do. He may have called you to be a missionary, pastor, doctor, teacher, athlete, dentist, entrepreneur (someone who owns their own business), stay at home mom, or musician. Whatever He's called you to do, He will give you the skill set to do it. You will also have a desire to do it. If your dog sings better than you and you hate to sing, then you know that you aren't going to grow up and become a singer.

On the other hand, maybe you love cooking, and everyone says your creations are delicious. You may one day become a famous chef or own a restaurant. No matter what God has called you to do, you have a part in seeing that it happens. He gave us a free will so it won't just automatically happen.

Gabby Douglas was the first black girl in history to win an individual all-around Olympic Games competition. She was only 16 years old at the time! Even though she was young, she had obstacles to overcome before she could become an Olympian. Gabby overcame being homeless and having a life-threatening illness at a young age. She acknowledged that God had given her the talent to be a gymnast. Gabby did not become a famous athlete by sitting on the couch, wishing. It took her recognizing the talent God had given her and lots of hard work and training.

At this point in your life, you may not know what God has called you to do. That's ok. You have time to figure it out, but there are steps that you need to take. First, you need to ask him. Spend time talking to Him about the plans that He has for you. Then, you need to listen to what He says. God talks to us through the inward witness. That's God's Spirit speaking to our spirit. It's like a spiritual feeling on the inside. If you have a good feeling about something on the inside, then that's a yes. If you have a yucky feeling on the inside about something, then that's a no. For example, maybe you're in high school, and you've been praying about if you should go to college or start your own business. You may think that college is the only way to make a good living, so your head is telling you to go, but when you pray about going to college, you have a yucky feeling on the inside.

On the other hand, when you pray about turning your hobby into a business, you have a good feeling. That's God leading you to leave college alone and take a step of faith and start that business. The more time you spend with God, the more you'll be able to recognize His voice.

Don't worry about your future. God will direct your steps if you follow Him. His plan comes in steps. If He were to show you everything that He wanted you to do, you would be overwhelmed and probably run and hide. Let your life be an adventure with God. It'll be the best adventure you can ever take.

Prayer for Child: Dear Heavenly Father, I ask you to direct my steps. I thank You that I hear your voice and every step I take is a step closer to You and everything You have for me. In Jesus name, Amen.

Prayer for Parent: Dear Heavenly Father, I'm so glad that You are directing my steps and that I'm on the right path. I ask You to show my children the path that You have for them. I thank You for directing their paths. In Jesus name, Amen.

CHALLENGE: Play a game of Follow the Leader or Simon Says as a family. Note to parents: Talk with your children about how this game relates to us following God.

DAY 19

YOU ARE AN OVERCOMER

"For everyone born of God is victorious *and* overcomes the world, and this is the victory that has conquered *and* overcome the world—our [continuing, persistent] faith [in Jesus the Son of God]."

1 John 5:4-5 AMP

The word overcome means to conquer or defeat. This Bible verse says that if you're born of God, then you are victorious and overcome the world. What does that mean? How do you overcome the world? Do you try to take over the world?

Let's think about what's in the world. Sickness is in the world. You don't have to look far to find someone who isn't well. Poverty is in the world. There's a lot of people who don't have enough food, money or a place to live. Hate is in the world. Some people hate other people just because they have a different skin color than them. There are temptations in the world. Temptation is when you have an urge to do something that God says is wrong. What God is saying in the above scripture, is that through Him, we can conquer or defeat any problem that tries to come into our world.

School was not easy for Jason. He struggled with his grades, and retaining information was hard for him. Jason knew that he had a Spelling test on Friday, and he was very nervous that he was going to fail it. He studied the best he could but still felt that it wasn't enough. Soon it was Friday and Jason was shaking in his boots. He wanted to spend the weekend at Mark's house, but Jason's parents had told him that if he failed his test, he couldn't go. As the teacher called out the words, Jason noticed that he could see Rachel's paper. Rachel was a smart girl that always made A's. Jason knew that it was wrong to cheat, but he was having a battle within himself. "What should I do?" he thought. In an instant, Jason decided to do what he knew God would want him to do. He turned his head so that he could no longer see Rachel's paper and asked the Lord to help him. Jason's teacher called him to her desk at the end of the day. Jason thought that he had failed his test. His teacher said, "Jason, I'm very proud of you. You made a B+." Jason was so excited! He had overcome the temptation to cheat, and by studying and relying on the Lord to help him, he had made a good grade.

You are an overcomer because the Lord says that you are. You can overcome any problem or situation with His help. God always has the solutions to any problem that we may face. Start thinking and seeing yourself as an overcomer today!

Prayer for Child: Dear Heavenly Father, I'm so thankful that you have made me an overcomer. I ask you to help me conquer any problem that I may face. In Jesus name, Amen.

Prayer for Parent: Dear Heavenly Father, I thank You for making me victorious and able to overcome every situation that I may encounter. In Jesus name, Amen.

CHALLENGE: Write a story or draw a picture that features you as an overcomer. Your story or drawing can be about a real-life situation or made up. Let your imagination run wild!

Examples of imaginary stories: You're a knight slaying a dragon, or you're a princess warrior rescuing orphans.

Examples of real-life situations: You're not feeling well, so you pray and all the symptoms you had disappeared.

DAY 20

YOU ARE CONFIDENT

"But blessed are those who trust in the Lord and have made the Lord their hope and confidence."

Jeremiah 17:7 NLT

Confident: Sure of oneself, having no uncertainty about one's own abilities, correctness, successfulness, bold

God created you in His image. He wants you to walk around with your head up, knowing that you are His child. God wants you to be able to look people in the eye and speak in front of people without feeling like you're not good enough. He wants you to be sure of yourself. I didn't say full of yourself. God wants you to be confident but not cocky. Confidence and arrogance are not the same things. Confident people believe that they are equal to other people. Arrogant people believe that they are better than other people. The Lord wants you to make Him your confidence. You can be confident because your confidence comes from Him. That means that you can be sure of yourself because He is sure of you.

In the book of Esther, we read about a woman who was confident because she put her trust in the Lord. Esther was an orphan girl who was chosen by King Xerxes to be his Queen. He did not know that she was a Jewish girl. Esther's uncle had raised her and worked in the king's palace. He told her not to tell the king that she was Jewish.

The king appointed a man named Haman to a special position in his kingdom and ordered all the servants to bow down to him. When Esther's uncle, Mordecai, refused to bow down to him, it made Haman mad. It made him so mad that he went to the king and told him that the Jews did not obey his laws. He convinced the king to issue a decree saying that he would give 10,000 talents of silver to anyone who would kill the Jews. In ancient Persia, when the king made a decree and sealed it with his signet ring (a ring with letters, usually one's initials, or a design carved into it) it could not change.

Mordecai told Esther that she must go before the king and stop this. The king had a rule that no one could come before him unless he invited them to come. Not even his wife! If they did come to him, they would be killed unless he held out his golden scepter (a staff carried by rulers.) Esther decided to go to him and ask him not to kill the Jews. When she walked in, the King held out the scepter. In the end, the Jews were saved from death.

Only a confident woman would walk into a room, knowing that the penalty was death. Esther was confident that the king wouldn't kill her because she put her confidence in the Lord. That is what allowed her to walk into that room with her head held high. She knew who she was and who she was representing. So today as you go about your daily routine, go out with your head held high knowing that you are a daughter or son of the King.

Prayer for Child: Dear Heavenly Father, I thank You that I am confident because I know who I am in You. In Jesus name, Amen.

Prayer for Parent: Dear Heavenly Father, I thank You that I am confident in leading my family, I'm confident in my job, and I'm a confident person. I put my hope and confidence in You. In Jesus name, Amen.

CHALLENGE: Act out the story of Esther as a family or write your own story about being confident and act it out.

DAY 21

YOU ARE STRONG IN THE LORD

"Finally, my brethren, be strong in the Lord and in the power of His might. Put on the whole armor of God, that you may be able to stand against the wiles of the devil."

Ephesians 6:10 NKJV

One of my favorite superheroes is Iron Man. I love his red and gold suit. Iron Man's suit is awesome! It can do so many things, but it has one main purpose. Iron Man's suit was created to protect him. His suit, made from strong materials, keep him safe. It's his protective armor. Another cool aspect of Iron Man's suit is that it makes him strong. He can lift 100 tons! That's the equivalent of 200 elephants!

God wants us to be strong like Iron Man. Just like Iron Man has an armor that he puts on, God has an armor that He wants us to put on. When we put on God's armor, it protects us from evil, and it makes us strong. Our armor is cooler than Iron Man's because it's invisible. We know that we have it on, but no one else can see it.

Iron Man's armor is powerful, but if he didn't put it on, it wouldn't do him any good. We're the same way. To get our armor to work, we must put it on, but we can't put it on until we know what it is.

Let's take a look at our armor:

Helmet of Salvation

You put this on when you ask Jesus into your heart.

The Belt of Truth

The belt of truth is knowing the truth of God's promises found in His word.

The Breastplate of Righteousness

The breastplate goes on our chest and protects our heart. We put on the breastplate of righteousness by keeping our hearts clean and knowing that we are right with God.

The Shoes of Peace

These shoes allow us to have peace no matter where we go or what we face.

The Sheild of Faith

The sheild of faith will protect you from any missile that the devil tries to launch at you.

The Sword of the Spirit

The sword of the spirit is your Bible. Read it and get God's Word on the inside of you.

Now that you know what the armor is, you are ready to put it on. I've already told you that it's invisible, so how can you put on something that you can't see? We put our armor on every day by praying, worshipping God, and reading the Bible. Get up every morning and put your armor on. Don't get caught without it!

Prayer for Child: Dear Heavenly Father, I thank You that I'm strong in You. I will put on my armor every day so that I can stand firm against the devil's evil plans. In Jesus name, Amen.

Prayer for Parent: Dear Heavenly Father, I thank You that I'm strong in You and the power of Your might. I put on the whole armor so that I can stand against the wiles of the devil. I will watch and pray so that Your plans are accomplished in my life and my family. In Jesus name, Amen.

CHALLENGE: Name your armor without looking back at the devotion. Then draw a picture of yourself as a superhero. What kind of armor will you wear?

DAY 22

YOU ARE A BOY/GIRL OF INTEGRITY

"People with integrity walk safely, but those who follow crooked paths will be exposed."

Proverbs 10:9 NLT

"The Lord detests lying lips, but he delights in those who tell the truth."

Proverbs 12:22 NLT

"Choose a good reputation over great riches; being held in high esteem is better than silver or gold."

Proverbs 22:1 NLT

Integrity: the quality of being honest and having strong moral principles

I want you to close your eyes and think about the most honest person that you know. Then, I want you to think about someone you know that never tells the truth. Now, open your eyes. There was probably one person that stood out in your mind and matched each of these descriptions. God says that a good reputation is better than riches. Today's devotion is about integrity. Integrity is who you are when no one else is watching.

Xavier loved all kinds of sweets, but cookies were his favorite. His mom had a rule that he could have one cookie after supper every night if he ate all his dinner. One night, Xavier came down the stairs for dinner to find a plate full of chicken and broccoli. He liked chicken, but he thought broccoli was the worst vegetable ever! Xavier chose not to eat the broccoli, so his mom reminded him that he couldn't have a cookie after dinner. Xavier wanted a cookie! Later that night, Xavier snuck in the kitchen. He eyed the cookie jar. Mom and Dad were watching tv in the living room and probably wouldn't even hear the jar open. Xavier quickly took one cookie and snuck back upstairs. The next day, while Xavier's mom was putting his laundry away, she noticed cookie crumbs by his bed. When Xavier got home from school, his mom confronted him about the cookie crumbs. Xavier admitted what he had done and received his punishment, no cookies and x box for two weeks. The worst part was that his mom and dad no longer trusted him. He would have to earn their trust again.

God is always watching. He sees everything and knows everything. You can never fool Him. Always be honest and do what is right. If you learn to be an honest kid, you will grow up to be an honest adult. God created you to be a person of integrity.

Prayer for Child: Dear Heavenly Father, I ask You to help me always to tell the truth and do what's right. I want people to see Jesus in me. I will strive to please You in everything I do. In Jesus name, Amen.

Prayer for Parent: Dear Heavenly Father, I ask You to help me be a man/woman of integrity. I thank You that I always do the right thing even when no one is looking. I know that nothing is hidden from You. I ask You to help me model a lifestyle of integrity in front of my family. In Jesus name, Amen.

CHALLENGE: Play a game of "What Would You Do?"

Instructions:

1. Choose a child to go first.
2. Parent asks the child a question.
3. Child answers.
4. Take turns until all children have played.

Questions:

1. You find a wallet in a public restroom. What would you do?

2. You forgot to study for a test. During the test, you can see your neighbor's answers. What do you do?

3. Your parents grounded you from video games, but they forgot to take your PS4 out of your room. What do you do?

Now, make up your own questions. Let the children come up with their own scenarios.

DAY 23

YOU ARE A LIGHT IN THE DARKNESS

"For you were once darkness, but now you are light in the Lord. Walk as children of light."

Ephesians 5:8 NKJV

"Then Jesus spoke to them again saying, "I am the light of the world. He who follows Me shall not walk in darkness, but have the light of life."

John 8:14 NKJV

Fireflies are fascinating insects. They are glow in the dark bugs! As a child, I used to catch them and store them in a jar; but fireflies were not created to be kept in a jar. They were created to shine! Just like fireflies light up the night, God wants us to be a light to others that are living in darkness.

Jesus is the light of the world. When you accept Him as your Savior, you are delivered from darkness. Darkness is sin. Sin is doing the opposite of what God says to do. It's when you do wrong even though you know to do right.

People who are living in darkness are lost because they can't see.

Have you ever tried to walk around your house in the dark? Maybe you can because it's familiar to you, but what if you tried to walk around a friend's house without any light. It would be very difficult. You would probably bump into a lot of things and get lost. God wants us to help people, lost in darkness, by being a light. If we let our light shine, it will lead people to Him.

You are never too young or too old to let your light shine. The best way to let our light shine is by living our life for Jesus. When we act and talk like Jesus, people lost in darkness will notice. You have something that they want. You're different! People, lost in darkness, are sad, lonely, and mad. As a Christian, you should be happy, loving, and glad. Show the love of God to everyone you meet. You never know who is lost in darkness and needs someone to lead them to Jesus.

Prayer for Child: Dear Heavenly Father, I thank You for calling me into the light. I ask you to help me be a light in the darkness so that I can lead others to You. In Jesus name, Amen.

Prayer for Parent: Dear Heavenly Father, I'm so thankful that You saved me from the powers of darkness. I thank You that I'm set free from sin. I will let my light shine for You. I ask You to send the unsaved, hurting and backslider across my path so that I can lead them to You. In Jesus name, Amen.

CHALLENGE: Talk about how you can be a light in your everyday life.

Example 1: A new student comes to your school. You shine your light by being friendly to him/her.

Example 2: The teacher tells everyone not to talk in class. You shine your light by not talking.

DAY 24

YOU ARE A PRAY-ER

"If you believe, you will receive what you ask for when you pray."

Matthew 21:22 NIRV

"You may ask me for anything in my name. I will do it."

John 14:14 NIRV

Do you have a best friend? If so, do you talk to him/her every day? What if you went for a week or a month without talking to them. You would probably start to think that they didn't want to be your best friend anymore. Some people will talk to their best friend every day, but go days and weeks without talking to God. God wants to be number one in your life. He wants you to have great relationships with your family and friends, but He wants your most important relationship to be with Him. Prayer is how we communicate with God. We may not see Him, but we can still hear Him, and He hears us.

George Muller lived in the 1800s. He was a Christian evangelist and missionary who took care of orphans. He was a man of faith. When he prayed, He knew God would answer his prayers. On one occasion, the house mother of the orphanage told George Muller that the kids were dressed and ready for school, but there was no food in the house. He told her to take the 300 children into the dining room and have them to sit at the tables. He prayed and thanked God for the food and waited. Within minutes, a baker knocked on the door. The baker said," Mr. Muller, last night I could not sleep. Somehow, I knew that you would need bread this morning. I got up and baked three batches for you. I will bring it in." Then there was another knock at the door. It was the milkman. His cart had broken down right in front of the orphanage. He asked if they could use some free milk because it would spoil by the time he got the wheel fixed. There was just enough milk for the 300 kids.

God doesn't just answer grown-up's prayers. He will answer your prayers too! When you pray, believe that you have what you asked for. Remember, God is not a genie in a magic lamp. He does want to give you nice things, but He wants your prayers to go beyond just asking for things for yourself. Also, the things you pray must be in line with His will. We know that His will is His Word. So, when you read your Bible, you will find out what to pray.

Here is an example of a silly prayer. "Dear God, please let me live at Disney World and eat chocolate cake for breakfast every day." That prayer would not happen because God gave you to parents that don't live in the castle at Disney World and eating chocolate cake for breakfast every day isn't good for you.

Here is an example of a good prayer. "Dear Heavenly Father, I thank you for this day. I thank You for giving me life. I thank You that I'm in good health. I plead the blood of Jesus over my family and myself today. I thank You for the angels that are around us and are keeping us safe. I pray for our President and leaders. I ask you to help them make good decisions. In Jesus name, Amen."

Talk to God the same way that you talk to your mom or dad. He loves you and can't wait to hear from you. God wants you to be a praying kid!

Challenge: Take turns praying. The more you pray, the more comfortable you will be doing it. Praying together will bring you closer to God and your family.

DAY 25

YOU ARE A PRAISER

"Praise the Lord. Praise God in His holy temple. Praise Him in His mighty heavens. Praise Him for His powerful acts. Praise Him because He is greater than anything else. Praise Him by blowing trumpets. Praise Him with harps and lyres. Praise Him with tambourines and dancing. Praise Him with stringed instruments and flutes. Praise Him with clashing cymbals. Praise Him with clanging cymbals. Let everything that has breath praise the Lord. Praise the Lord."

Psalm 150:1-6 NIRV

"Celebrate God all day, every day."

Philippians 4:4 MSG

When you think of praising God, the first thing that comes to your mind is probably singing at church. While this is one way to praise God, it's not the only way.

Praise means to tell or show God how much we love Him and how thankful we are for everything He does for us. There are different ways to praise God. We can praise Him through singing, playing an instrument, dancing, or by telling Him how great He is and expressing how much we love Him.

Praising God should be a part of your everyday life. I love the Message translation of Philippians 4:4. We should celebrate God all day, every day. Without Him, we wouldn't be alive! When you wake up in the morning, the first thing you should do is praise the Lord. Thank Him for waking you up and tell him how much you love Him.

In 2 Samuel 6, David praised God by dancing before Him with all his might. He danced so hard that his clothes fell off! His wife was embarrassed. One translation said that when she saw him, she hated him in her heart. She was more concerned about what people thought of them than she was with pleasing God. Never be ashamed to praise God and never be ashamed when someone you know praises God. David's wife paid the price for being ashamed of him. She never had any kids.

Praise comes from the heart. If you have not been praising God, today is a good time to start. At first, it may feel awkward, but the more you praise God, the more comfortable you will become doing it. If you have breath and are alive and breathing, then you should praise the Lord.

Prayer for Child: Dear Heavenly Father, I praise you because you are a good, good Father. I'll never be ashamed to praise you! I can lift my hands, sing, and play for you with freedom because I'm glad to be your child. I thank you that my praises will be a sweet sound in your ear. In Jesus name, Amen.

Prayer for Parent: Dear Heavenly Father, I praise you with all that is in me. Your praise is always on my lips! I can lift my hands, sing, and play for you with freedom. I'll never be ashamed to praise you because of all you've done for me. I thank you for inhabiting my praises. In Jesus name, Amen.

Challenge: Turn on your favorite praise and worship song and praise God together as a family. If your family plays instruments, then play and sing to the Lord.

DAY 26

YOU ARE FORGIVING

"And when you stand praying, if you hold anything against anyone, forgive them, so that your Father in heaven may forgive you your sins."

Mark 11:25 NIV

"Put up with each other. Forgive the things you are holding against one another. Forgive, just as the Lord forgave you."

Colossians 3:13 NIRV

When someone does you wrong, it makes you sad or mad. You usually want to get even and make the person feel the hurt that you are experiencing. Seeking revenge is not God's way of doing things. He commands us to forgive anyone who does us wrong.

In the book of Matthew, Peter (one of Jesus' disciples) asked Jesus how many times he should forgive someone. He thought that seven times should be enough. Jesus responded and told him that he should forgive someone 70 x 7. That's a lot of times! The point Jesus was making is that we should always forgive.

Some people find it difficult to forgive others because they still feel hurt by what someone else did to them. Jesus can help you erase the hurt in your heart.

When you forgive someone, you're not saying that what the other person did was ok; you're just choosing not to let the wrongdoing affect you anymore. You're also choosing not to hold their crime against them.

Forgiveness is a decision. It's not a feeling. We forgive others so that God will forgive us. The way you know that you have truly forgiven someone is when you can think about that person without any bad or sad feelings. If someone says that person's name and you get mad, then you haven't truly forgiven them.

Christians are to be imitators of God. That means that we should act like Him. God is always faithful to forgive us, so we should forgive others.

Prayer for Child: Dear Heavenly Father, I'm so thankful that you forgive me when I mess up. I ask you to help me to forgive others who have done me wrong. I am always quick to forgive. In Jesus name, Amen.

Prayer for Parent: Dear Heavenly Father, I thank you that you are faithful to forgive me of all my sin. I forgive others just as you have forgiven me. I never hold grudges, and I'm quick to forgive others. In Jesus name, Amen.

CHALLENGE: Get a piece of paper and write down the name of anyone you need to forgive. It may be a long list, or it may be a short list. Pray from your heart and tell the Lord that you choose to forgive that person or those people. Then, tear the paper up and throw it away. You are no longer holding a record of their wrongs!

DAY 27

YOU ARE KIND

"And be ye kind one to another, tenderhearted, forgiving one another, even as God for Christ's sake hath forgiven you."

Ephesians 4:32 KJV

Wow! There's another verse about forgiveness, but we're going to be focusing on the first part of this scripture today. It says to be kind and tenderhearted to one another.

Someone kind and tenderhearted is considered to be good-natured, friendly, caring, and thoughtful. Everyone knows that one person who is so sweet. It just seems like it's their personality to be sweet. Everyone likes them. They have a lot of friends, and being kind comes easy to them. So, should the rest of us not be kind because it doesn't come naturally to us? No!

Susie was in the fifth grade. She was smart, pretty, and oh, so sweet. She earned the nickname Sweet Susie one day after she gave her lunch to a kid who had dropped his. Every day just seemed like rainbows and sunshine for Sweet Susie. Her circle of friends was always expanding, and she never had to worry about being picked last to participate in any group activity.

Rick was also in the fifth grade. He was cool, witty, and always had something funny to say even if it was at the expense of others. He too had a nickname, Slick Rick. Slick Rick had his circle of friends and wasn't interested in the opinions of others. Some kids loved Rick's sense of humor, and others thought he was a bully. Rick loved people thinking that he was a tuff guy. He thought showing kindness was for women and preachers.

Our behavior and thoughts are a combination of our God-given personality and our environment. We tend to model the behavior of our family. In this scenario, Sweet Susie grew up as an only child with kind parents. Slick Rick was the youngest of three older brothers and had to learn how to take up for himself.

God requires certain things of us, no matter our background. He wants us to spend time with Him and take on his characteristics. God is kind, and He tells us to be kind.

It may take some work for you to be kind. It's hard to be kind to someone who is mean, but you can do it with the Lord's help.

Think of ways that you can show kindness to the people around you. Sharing is one way to show kindness. You may have a cookie, and your brother wants some. Give him half. There's a lot of ways to show kindness.

Remember, you are the only Jesus that some people will ever see. Your actions will either point them to Christ or push them away. A little kindness can go a long way.

"In a world where you can be anything, be kind."- Unknown

Prayer for Child: Dear Heavenly Father, I ask you to help me always to show your kindness to others. I am kind because you are kind. In Jesus name, Amen.

Prayer for Parent: Dear Heavenly Father, I thank you for always being kind to me. You're kind, even when I'm not. Help me to be kind so that I exemplify who You are. In Jesus name, Amen.

Challenges:

1. Parents: Have your kids explain in their own words what it means to be kind. Ask them if anyone has been unkind to them. At this time, discuss bullying. Your child may have been bullied, is being bullied, or has participated in bullying someone else. Have an open and honest conversation and help them deal with whatever problem they are having.

2. Today, find a way to show an act of kindness to someone.

DAY 28

YOU ARE PEACEFUL

"Let the peace that Christ gives rule in your hearts. As parts of one body, you were appointed to live in peace. And be thankful."

Colossians 3:15 NIRV

"Turn all your worries over to Him. He cares about you."

1 Peter 5:7 NIRV

With every new day, there is a new opportunity to let things bother you and make you upset. It can be a small thing like your brother smacking his cereal in the morning, or it can be a big thing like losing your pet. No matter what we face, God says that we are to let the peace that Christ gives rule in our hearts.

The peace of God is a calmness that comes on us when we put our trust in God. It is freedom from upsetting thoughts or feelings. The way that we experience God's peace is by turning our worries over to Him. It's an exchange process. We give Him our worries, and in return, He gives us peace.

Is there a place or an activity that brings you peace? Some

people find peace at the beach from watching the waves of the ocean. Some people find it in the mountains being surrounded by nature. When I float on my back in a pool with the sun shining down on me, I feel peace. The combination of the coolness of the water and the warmth of the sun brings a feeling that soothes my soul. It's good to have a place or an activity that makes you feel peaceful, but those things can't compare to the peace that the Lord gives.

God's peace in your heart makes every situation possible to endure because you rest in Him. You know that you will always be ok no matter what life may throw at you.

Prayer for Child: Dear Heavenly Father, I give all my worries to you because I know you care for me. I will let your peace rule in my heart every day of my life. In Jesus name, Amen.

Prayer for Parent: Dear Heavenly Father, I cast all my cares on you for I know you care for me. I let your peace rule in my heart no matter what situation comes my way. I put my trust in you because you're a good and loving Father. In Jesus name, Amen.

CHALLENGE: The Hebrew word Shalom means peace be with you. The Jewish people use it as a greeting when saying hello or goodbye, but it has a greater meaning. Shalom means completeness and wholeness in every area of our life. When you speak the word Shalom to someone, you are delivering God's message of peace to them. When you say Shalom to a family member, you are saying, "I choose to let God bring peace to this relationship."

Write a letter to a family member using the greeting Shalom.

DAY 29

YOU ARE A PEACEMAKER

"Blessed are those that make peace. They will be called the sons of God."

Matthew 5:9 NIRV

A house that is on fire needs something to put it out. Can you guess what it is? That's right! Water! If you wanted the house to continue to burn and make the flames higher, then what would you throw on it? You guessed it, gasoline!

The Bible says that Christians are to be peacemakers. A peacemaker is someone who brings a calmness or unity to a situation. Every day you carry around two invisible buckets. One bucket is full of water, and the other is full of gasoline. You can choose to start fires or put them out.

There are two types of people, firefighters and fire starters. A firefighter is always looking for a solution to a problem. No matter how big the fire, he never gives up. A fire starter is always causing problems. They tend to be people who are always disagreeable and selfish.

TJ, Ashley, and Camden were cousins. They loved to play together, but sometimes TJ and Camden didn't get along. They were both the oldest in their families, and they loved to be in charge. One afternoon, while hanging out at their grandparent's house, TJ and Camden got into a heated argument. "Let's play kickball!" TJ yelled. "No, I don't like kickball. Let's play basketball instead," exclaimed Camden. "You just don't want to play kickball because you know I'm better than you!", cried TJ. "No, it's not that. You think you should always get to pick what we play," said Camden. Ashley could feel things getting tense and was starting to get uncomfortable. She didn't want to get in the middle of the boy's argument, but she remembered the lesson she had learned in church the week before. Mr. Andrew had taught on being a peacemaker. She thought for a moment, then spoke up and said, "Let's play kickball for 15 minutes and then play basketball for 15 minutes? That way, you both get to play what you want." The boys stopped arguing and decided that was a great idea.

In our story, Ashley chose to be a peacemaker, aka firefighter. There was a problem (fire), and she chose to put it out with her words. She had three choices. She could've walked away without saying anything, she could've made the situation worse by choosing sides, or she could've offered a solution. She chose to offer a solution to the problem. By offering a solution, she brought unity to the two boys.

Will you be a firefighter or a fire starter? I hope you choose to be a firefighter.

Prayer for Child: Dear Heavenly Father, I ask you to forgive me for the times that I've chosen to be a fire starter. I want to be a peacemaker so that I can please you. I ask you to help me respond to every situation the way that you would. In Jesus name, Amen.

Prayer for Parent: Dear Heavenly Father, I ask you to forgive me for the times that I've chosen not to be a peacemaker. I ask for your wisdom in every situation so that I always know the right thing to do and say. In Jesus name, Amen.

CHALLENGE: Create scenarios where you would need to be a peacemaker and act them out.

DAY 30

YOU ARE HUMBLE

"....Wherefore he saith, God resisteth the proud, but giveth grace unto the humble."

James 4:6 KJV

"Humble yourselves in the sight of the Lord, and he shall lift you up."

James 4:10 KJV

Humble- having or showing a modest or low estimate of one's own importance.

Have you ever been around someone who loved to brag? They want to convince you that what they have or who they are is better than you or anyone else. Another word for brag is to boast. Boast means to talk with excessive pride and self-satisfaction about one's achievements, possessions, or abilities.

People boast about different things, how much one paid for something, their car, their singing ability, how much money they make, their athletic ability, and their looks.

They want all the attention to be on them.

The people that I am describing are full of pride. In other words, they have a big head! They think that they're on top and everyone else is at the bottom. They haven't taken the time to realize that God is the one who gives talents and abilities. The Bible says that God resists the proud. Prideful people are not pleasing to the Lord.

Our second scripture says that if you humble yourself in the sight of the Lord that He will lift you up. That means that if you will acknowledge that God is the one who gave you your ability, wealth, or talent that He will cause you to have great success and everyone will notice.

Tim Tebow is a man with a lot of athletic ability. He humbled himself before the Lord, and the Lord caused him to succeed. Tim was a homeschooler that worked hard to play football with the public school. He didn't walk on the field and talk about how great he was. He served the Lord lifted him up. Today he is a successful athlete.

If you are feeling the need to brag on yourself, then you probably feel like you lack attention or importance. Dear sweet child, you are so valuable and loved by your Father God. You are the apple of His eye! God knows how special you are because He made you that way. Spend time with Him, and you'll soon realize it too.

Prayer for Child: Dear Heavenly Father, I ask you to forgive me for times that I've boasted. I acknowledge that everything I am and all that I have is because of you. From this day forward, I will be humble and let you lift me up. In Jesus name, Amen.

Prayer for Parent: Dear Heavenly Father, I ask you to forgive me for the times that I've been prideful. I acknowledge that everything I am and all that I have is because of you. Without you, I am nothing. From this day forward, I will be humble and let you lift me up. In Jesus name, Amen.

CHALLENGE: God sometimes uses other people to lift you up. Take turns giving each other compliments. Make sure that they are from your heart.

DAY 31

YOU ARE COURAGEOUS

"Be strong and courageous, do not be afraid or tremble in dread before them, for it is the Lord your God who goes with you. He will not fail you or abandon you."

Deuteronomy 31:6 AMP

You were made to be courageous. When you go about your life full of courage, nothing can stop you. Courage allows you to face hard things without fear. Courage means that you are brave. As a Christian, our courage comes from putting our trust in the Lord, knowing that He will always watch over us.

Let's read Joshua 1:1-9 (NIRV)

Moses, the servant of the Lord, died. After that, the Lord spoke to Joshua, the son of Nun. Joshua was Moses' helper. The Lord said to Joshua, "My servant Moses is dead. Now then, I want you and all of these people to get ready to go across the Jordan River. I want all of you to go into the land I am about to give to the people of Israel.

I will give all of you every place you walk on, just as I promised Moses. Your territory will reach from the Negev Desert all the way to Lebanon. The great Euphrates River will be to the east. The Mediterranean Sea will be to the west. Your territory will include all of the Hittite country.

Joshua, no one will be able to stand up against you as long as you live. I will be with you, just as I was with Moses. I will never leave you. I will never desert you.

Be strong and brave. You will lead these people, and they will take the land as their very own. It is the land I promised with an oath to give their people long ago.

Be strong and very brave. Make sure you obey the whole law my servant Moses gave you. Do not turn away from it to the right or the left. Then you will have success wherever you go.

Never stop reading this Scroll of the Law. Day and night you must think about what it says. Make sure you do everything that is written in it. Then things will go well with you. And you will have great success.

Here is what I command you to do. Be strong and brave. Do not be terrified. Do not lose hope. I am the Lord your God. I will be with you everywhere you go."

Wow! The Lord told Joshua 3 times in these verses to be

strong and brave. Other translations say courageous. God knew Joshua was going to have to be courageous to carry out His plan. Moses had died, and God made Joshua the new leader. Joshua was to lead the people into the Promised Land. The Israelites had been wandering in the desert for 40 years, but it was time to take the land. Joshua knew that is was going to be a challenge to get to the promised land. It was a scary task! There was real danger! He would face armies and giants in the land, but God told Joshua not to be afraid and have courage. Joshua put his trust in the Lord and chose to be courageous and not to fear. In the end, he led the people into the Promised Land.

Did you notice in the story that God told Joshua that no one would be able to stand against him as long as he was alive because He would be with him? He had a promise from God. But God also gave him some instructions. He told Joshua to obey the whole law that Moses gave him and to not turn from it. God was telling him not to do it his way. We get in trouble when we try to do things our way instead of God's way.

God will always be with you the same way that He was with Joshua. Whatever he tells you to do, go after it. Don't ever be scared because the Lord is on your side. If He calls you to it, He'll take you through it. He will never fail you or leave you.

Prayer for Child: Dear Heavenly Father, I won't fear when things seem scary or hard because you told me to be courageous. I'm brave because I know that you're on my side and that you'll never leave me. I follow after you and obey your Word. I will read your Word and hide it in my heart so that I always have the answers to any of life's problems, and I will face them with courage. In Jesus name, Amen.

Prayer for Parent: Dear Heavenly Father, I have courage because I am confident that you will see me through any difficulties or trials. I embrace your plan for my life, and I'll run my race courageously. I won't back down when things don't come easy because I know that you will always be on my side, leading me to victory. I am a student of the Word. I study your Word so that I will know the answers to any of life's problems, and I will face them with courage. In Jesus name, Amen.

CHALLENGE: It takes courage to sing in front of people. It takes courage to speak in front of your class. It takes courage to shoot foul shots while the whole gym is staring at you. What do you need courage for? Make a list of the things that you need the Lord to give you the courage to do, and then step out in faith and do them. It may be hard at first, but the Lord will help you.

Matthew 5:14-16 KJV, "You are the light of the world. A city that is set on a hill cannot be hid. Neither do men light a candle, and put it under a bushel, but on a candlestick; and it giveth light unto all that are in the house. Let your light so shine before men, that they may see your good works, and glorify your Father which is in Heaven."

ABOUT THE AUTHOR

Rebekah Price

Rebekah Price is married to her high school sweetheart, Josh, and is a mom to four boys. She serves alongside her husband in Children's ministry at Faith Family Church in Jefferson, SC. She previously taught elementary school and is currently homeschooling the two youngest boys.

Made in the USA
Middletown, DE
20 July 2023

35009219R00056